Macmillan/McGraw-Hill READING

Contributors

The Princeton Review, Time Magazine, Accelerated Reader

The Princeton Review is not
affiliated with Princeton
University or ETS.

Students with print disabilities may be eligible to obtain an accessible, audio
version of the pupil edition of this textbook. Please call Recording for the Blind &
Dyslexic at 1-800-221-4792 for complete information.

Published by Macmillan/McGraw-Hill, a division of The McGraw-Hill Companies, Inc., Two Penn Plaza, NY, NY 10121

Printed in the United States of America

ISBN 0-02-188562-1/1, Bk.2

2 3 4 5 6 7 8 9 027/043 04 03 02

Macmillan/McGraw-Hill READING

Authors

James Flood

Jan E. Hasbrouck

James V. Hoffman

Diane Lapp

Donna Lubcker

Angela Shelf Medearis

Scott Paris

Steven Stahl

Josefina Villamil Tinajero

Karen D. Wood

**Macmillan
McGraw-Hill**

New York   Farmington

Together Is Better

Together Is Better

Cat Kisses

Sandpaper kisses
on a cheek or a chin—
that is the way
for a day to begin!

Sandpaper kisses—
a cuddle, a purr.
I have an alarm clock
that's covered with fur.

by Bobbi Katz

Tub Song

Rub, rub, rub-a-dub,

We are in the tub.

Hum, hum, we can sing.

We sing in the tub.

Fun, fun, we have fun.

A fun bath in the sun!

♡ Meet Frank Asch ♡

 Frank Asch discovered his love of writing and drawing when he was a boy. He wrote poems, plays, cartoons, and greeting cards. "I remember when I was just 13 or 14 making my first children's book for my sister," he says. Asch is now the author and illustrator of many award-winning children's books.

One Good Pup

by Frank Asch

You wish to go out, Pup.

You wish and wish.

But it is wet out.

It is so wet.

I wish to nap, Pup.
I can nap.

Can you nap?
Nap with me, Pup.

You wish to go out, Pup.
You wish and wish.

But it is wet out.

It is so wet.

Can you sit in this small ship, Pup?
Sit in this small ship with me.

You wish to go out, Pup.

But it is wet out.

I wish to play tug, Pup.
I can tug.

Can you tug?
Play tug with me, Pup.

You wish to go out, Pup.

You wish and wish.

But it is wet out.

It is so wet.

Can you sit?

Sit with me, Pup.

You wish to go out, Pup.

But it is wet out.

Can you mix, Pup?

Help me mix this, Pup.

Can you fish, Pup?

We can fish in the tub, Pup.

Can you ride, Pup?
Take a little ride, Pup.

This is fun for me.

It is no fun for Pup.

You are sad.
But you are not bad.

You are one good Pup!

1 What does the boy do with his pup?

2 Why doesn't he take the pup out?

3 What did you learn about pets?

4 Make up another title for the story.

5 Do you like Max or Pup better?

Write About Pup

Pretend Pup is yours.

Draw a picture.

Show you and Pup playing.

Write a sentence about your picture.

Make Raindrops

Draw a big raindrop.

Cut it out.

Draw something else the boy and Pup can do.

Find Out More

Find out more about dogs.

What do they eat?

How do you teach a dog?

Share what you learn.

A Picture Map

This is a picture map.

It shows Pup's back yard.

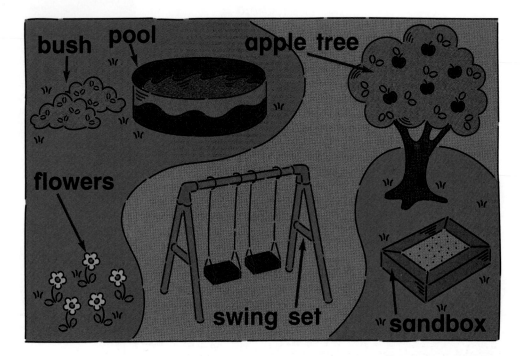

Look at the Map

❶ What is next to the pool?

❷ What is on the tree?

Sara and Her Pup

Sara has a new pup.

His name is Pal.

Sara likes Pal.

Sara shows Pal to her friends.

They like to play with Pal.

They think that Pal is fun.

How does Sara feel about Pal?

○ Sara thinks Pal is ugly.

○ Sara likes Pal.

What does the story tell you about feelings?

Jack-in-the-Box

Dot the Bug can hop, hop, hop.

She can hop to the bottom.

She can hop to the top.

She hops to the box.

The box goes POP!

Dot the Bug takes
a very big hop!

Meet Anne Miranda

As a child, Anne Miranda dreamed of becoming an artist. When she grew up, Miranda began writing stories. She says, "I found writing another way to put the pictures in my head down on paper, with words instead of color."

Meet Bernard Adnet

Bernard Adnet grew up in France. "I drew for many of my nieces and nephews when we were children," he says. Today he lives in New York and illustrates children's books.

The Bug Bath

by Anne Miranda

illustrated by Bernard Adnet

"We are very dirty," said Al.
"I want a bath," said Bob.

Al and Bob saw a big tub.

The two bugs got in.

The bath was hot.
But it was fun.

Bob kicked his legs.

Al sat in the suds.

A fish fell in the tub.
It got Bob and Al wet.

"We saw that," said Bob.
"You got us wet," said Al.

But the fish did not swim.
It just sat in the tub.

A big duck fell in the tub.
It landed on top of the bugs.

"We saw that," said Bob.

"You landed on us," said Al.

But the duck did not quack.
It just sat in the tub.

A big thud rocked the tub.
"What was that?" said the bugs.

"I see a leg," said Al.
"I see two legs," said Bob.

"What is it?" said Bob.

"It is a boy!" said Al.

"I want to get out!" said Bob.
"I want to run away!" said Al.

"Bugs!" said the boy.
Bob and Al dashed away.

Bob got on top of the fish.
The boy picked it up.

"A bug," he said.
"Let go!" said Bob.

Al got on top of the duck.

The boy picked it up.

"A bug," he said.
"Let go!" said Al.

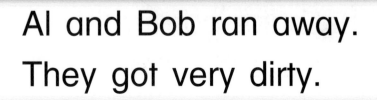

Al and Bob ran away.
They got very dirty.

"I see a bath," said Bob.
The bugs got in.

"We fit!" said Al.
"What a good bath for bugs!"
they said.

Story Questions & Activities

1. What fell in the tub?

2. What made them fall in the tub?

3. Why were the bugs afraid of the boy?

4. Tell the story's funny parts.

5. Have you read another story about bugs?

Write a Skit

Choose two bugs.
Write about what they say.

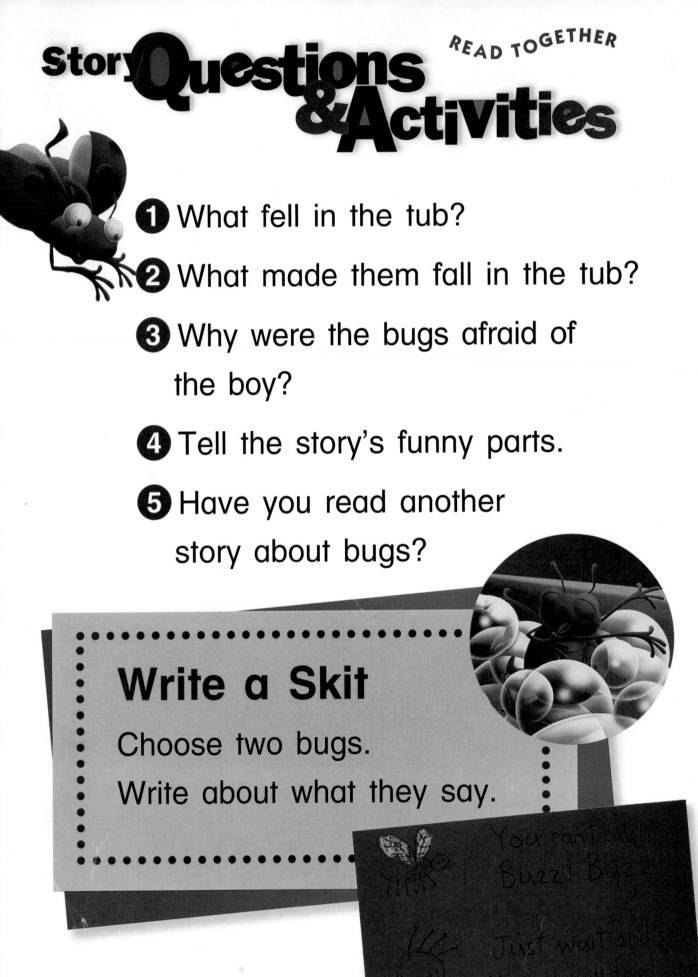

You can't catch me
Buzz! Buzz!

Just wait and see
My web will trap you

Make a Bug Puzzle

Draw a big bug on paper.

Cut it into small parts.

Ask a friend to put the parts together.

Find Out More

What is a spider?

Find out.

Share what you learn.

A Hippity-Hop Map

Maps tell how far apart things are.

Look at the Map

1 Start at the duck. How many hops to the boat?

2 Start at the boat. How many hops to the fish?

October 20

Dear Grandma,

Thank you for the new bath toys.

I like the duck and the fish.

They were very nice birthday gifts.

Thanks for coming to my party.

You are the best grandma!

Love, Ken

Ken's gifts make him feel –

○ happy

○ sad

What words in the story help you answer the question?

66

Pets

Jack has a duck and Meg
has a cat.

Jim has a pup that he calls Pat.

Ken has a fish that swims
in the tub.

And there is one small pig
in this club.

Big and small, pets are fun.

Pets, pets, pets for everyone.

Meet Jessica Clerk

When Jessica Clerk was a young girl, she liked to read and draw. Today, Clerk is a children's book author and illustrator.

Meet Ken Spengler

Ken Spengler says, "I always liked art, and I studied it a lot in school." He likes to make people see simple things in new and different ways.

Splash!

by Jessica Clerk

illustrated by Ken Spengler

It rained on the shed
and the big red barn.

"Good cat!" said Meg,
as she put on her hat.

"But my back and legs are wet,"
said Meg.

"It is not fun to be wet," said Meg.
"Not fun at all."

Then her hen ran up the path
with her red boots.

"Good hen!" said Meg,
as she put them on.

"But my back is wet, wet, wet," said Meg.

"It is not fun to be wet," said Meg. "Not fun at all."

Then her dog ran up the path
with her coat.

"Good dog!" said Meg,
as she put it on.

"I am not wet," said Meg.
"Not wet at all!"

It rained on Meg and on her pets.

Meg looked at her pets.
They were wet, wet, wet.

"It is not fun to be wet," said Meg.
"Not fun at all."

"I will be back," said Meg,
as she ran away down the path.

Meg went into the shed.
Then she went back to her pets.

When the bus came, there
were Meg and her pets.

And they were not wet at all!

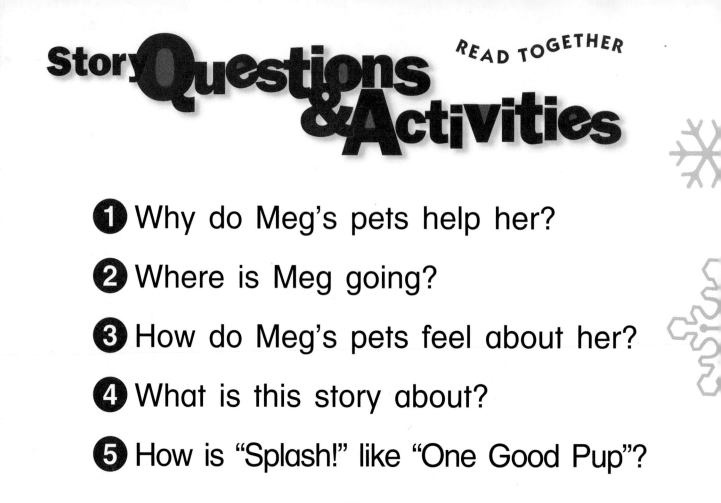

Story Questions & Activities

READ TOGETHER

1 Why do Meg's pets help her?

2 Where is Meg going?

3 How do Meg's pets feel about her?

4 What is this story about?

5 How is "Splash!" like "One Good Pup"?

Draw a Picture

Draw a picture.
Show yourself walking
in the rain.
What will you wear?

Make a Weather Calendar

Make a picture for the rain.

Make a picture for the sun.

Make a picture for the clouds.

Draw the pictures on a calendar.

Sunday	Monday	Tuesday	Wednesday	Thursday	Friday	Saturday

Find Out More

Find out how birds keep dry in the rain.

Meg's Footprint Map

Look at the Map

It shows the path Meg used to get her bag.

1 Did Meg go in and out the same door?

2 Where was her bag?

94

This Rain Hat

This is a rain hat.

This rain hat is a black hat.

It is on a rack.

Oh, no! It fell off the rack.

Now it is a flat hat.

It is a flat, black, rain hat.

What is this story about?

○ A hat that falls off the rack

○ A hat that a boy wears

Tell yourself the story in your own words.

Snacks

I sniff a great snack,

A snack on a sill.

Let me go and get my fill.

Slip me some bread,

Dip it in jam.

Then pass me a bit of that ham.

Meet Pat Cummings

When Pat Cummings was a child, she lived in many places in the United States and in other countries. Living in these places taught her to appreciate many different cultures. Today Cummings writes and illustrates books that celebrate people of many cultures.

What Bug Is It?

by
Pat Cummings

"Look around," said Miss Kim.
"You will see lots of bugs."

"I see a bug," said Rick.

"It is a small bug."

"It runs about on six legs and digs a hill," said Miss Kim.

"What bug is it?" said Rick.

"It is an ant!" said Jill.

"I see a bug," said Jill.

"It is red with black spots."

"Its wings pop up and snap shut again," said Miss Kim.

"Look!" said Jas.

"It is walking around on my hand."

"What bug is it?" said Jill.
"It is a ladybug!" said Nell.

"I see a bug," said Nell.
"I see a bug in a web."

"It is a bit fat," said Yan.
"But it has thin legs."

"It will use its web
to snag flies," said Miss Kim.

"What bug is it?" said Nell.
"It is a spider!" said Yan.

"I see a bug," said Yan.
"I see a bug flap its wings."

"It flies about and sips from flowers," said Miss Kim.

"There it is again!" said Rick.
"Now it looks slim and flat."

"What bug is it?" said Yan.

"It is a butterfly!" said Jas.

"Hush!" said Jas.
"What is that hum?"

"Let that bug pass!" said Jill.
"Do not smack at it."

"It will buzz," said Miss Kim.
"But let it do its job."

"What bug is it?" said Jas.

"It is a bee, so be careful!"
said Jill.

Story Questions & Activities

1 Which bug did Jill see?

2 Where does this story take place?

3 Why should bees be left alone?

4 What did you learn from this story?

5 Is this story like "The Bug Bath"?

Write a Riddle

Draw a picture of a bug.

Turn the drawing over.

Write a riddle about the bug.

Share it with the class.

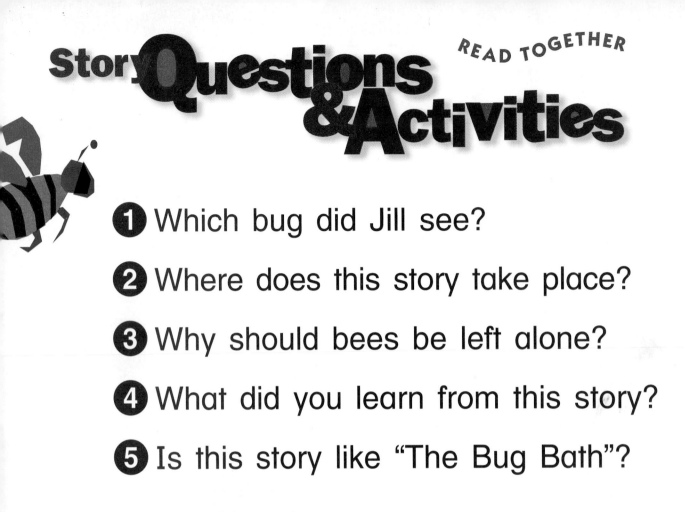

When it bites, I get an itch. What is it?

Sing a Song

Use pipe cleaners to make
a spider.

Then sing "Itsy Bitsy Spider."

Move your spider as you sing.

Find Out More

Learn how a caterpillar

turns into a butterfly.

Write about it.

A Street Map

A map helps us find our way.

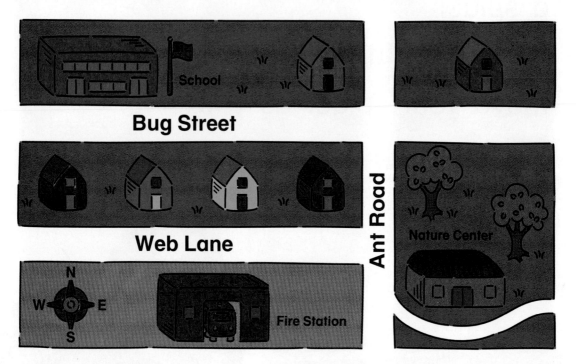

Look at the Map

1 On what street is the school?

2 Show how to get from the school to the nature center.

Honey Bees

It is summer.

The bees are buzzing.

They fly from flower to flower.

They get nectar from the flowers.

They make honey from the nectar.

We can eat honey.

It is good on toast.

It is good in tea.

In this story, what makes the honey?

○ The bees

○ The tea

Reading the story again can help you answer the question.

At the Vet

Muff the pup, Puff the cat,

And Sal the hog are at the vet.

Sal the hog is hot, so hot.

I will see that he drinks a lot.

Muff gets a shot, Puff gets a pill.

Now Muff and Puff will not get ill.

TIME
FOR KIDS
SPECIAL REPORT

A Vet

ALL PHOTOS UNLESS OTHERWISE NOTED BY KEN CAVANAGH

Do you have a pet?
A vet can care for it.

127

This vet helps big and small pets.
She can give a dog a checkup.

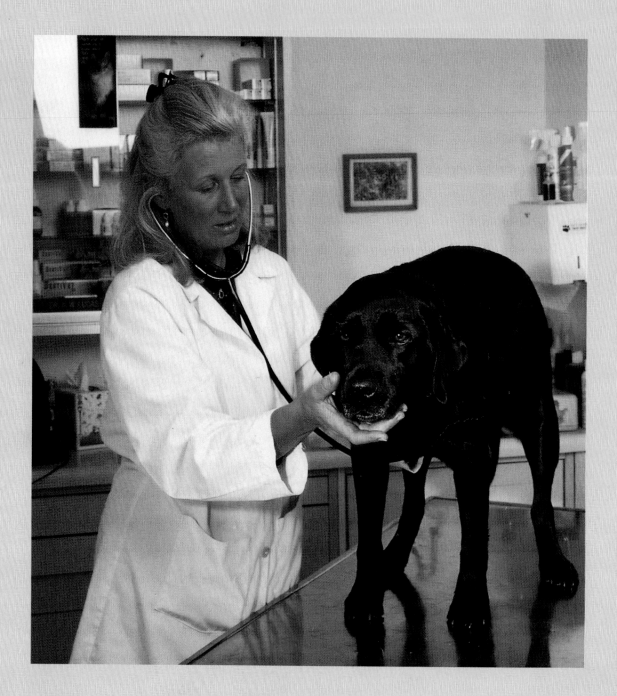

She can look at a duck.

She can look at a cat.

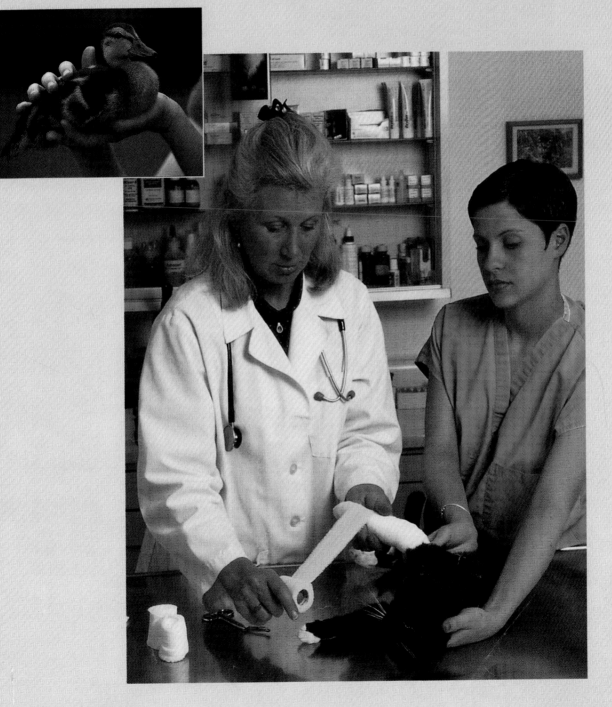

The vet can visit big pets.

She can look at a sick pig.

THIS PAGE: MARIO RUIZ

She can help out a horse.

This vet does a good job.

She wants to keep our pets well.

A story from the editors of *TIME FOR KIDS*.

Story Questions & Activities

READ TOGETHER

1. What pets does the vet help?

2. Where does this vet work at times?

3. Why do pets need a vet?

4. Tell what vets do.

5. Do any of these pets look like Meg's pets in "Splash"?

Make a List

Pretend you are a vet.
List pets you need to help.
Name each pet and tell each
one which day to come.

Monday	Tuesday	Wednesday	Thursday	Friday	Saturday	Sunday
Tim Cat	Dan Dog	Pat Pig	Pam Pup	Ron Rabbit		

Home Sweet Home

Use a shoebox.

Make a home for an animal.

Use things like twigs, leaves, and newspaper.

Find Out More

Find out one thing about vets who work in zoos.

STUDY SKILLS

Map

School

Luck Path

Sun Path

Pet Shop

VET

Look at the Map

1 What path will the girl take to get to the vet?

2 What is next to the vet's office?

Kim's Cat

Kim has a cat.

It is a very round cat.

Her vet says that it is like a ball.

Kim's cat rolls off the vet's table.

It rolls out the door.

Then, Kim's cat rolls all the way home.

What a silly cat!

In this story, what does the cat do?

○ Purrs when the vet holds it

○ Rolls off the vet's table

Think about what the story tells you.

138

Isn't It Strange?

Shoes have tongues,
But cannot talk;
Tables have legs,
But cannot walk;
Needles have eyes,
But cannot see;
Chairs have arms,
But they can't hug me!

by Leroy F. Jackson

Reading the Computer

We click on words and pictures to use the computer.

The Bug Bath

File	Cut	Copy	Print	Delete	Paste

The Bug Bath

I liked it when the duck fell in!

Computer Words and Pictures

Can you read these words and pictures?

= File

= Cut

= Print

= Copy

= Delete

= Paste

Questions

1 What does ✖ mean?

2 What does 🖨 let you do?

Glossary

This glossary can help you to find out the meanings of words in this book that you may not know.

The words are listed in alphabetical order. There is a picture and a simple sentence for each word. You can use the picture and sentence to help you understand the meaning of each word.

Sample Entry

Main Entry **Sample Sentence**

Butterfly

This is a beautiful **butterfly.**

Sample Picture

Boots

Jan's **boots** keep her feet dry.

Boy

There is one **boy** in the picture.
Another word for **boy** is *lad.*

Butterfly

This is a beautiful **butterfly.**

Cat

The **cat** likes to play with yarn.

Coat

My **coat** keeps me warm.

Dog

The **dog** is asleep.

Head

I put the hat on my **head.**

Hill

My house is on a **hill.**

Legs

A dog has four **legs.**

Nap

The baby is taking a **nap.**

Another word for **nap** is *rest*.

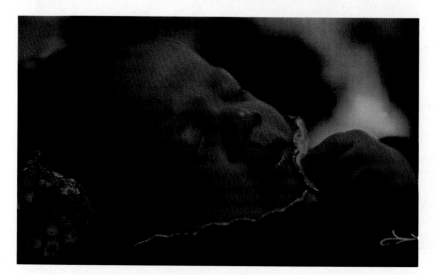

Pig

The **pig** stands on the grass.

Sit

The children **sit** and play.

Spider

The **spider** lives in a web.

Tub

I give my dog a bath in the **tub.**

Vet

The **vet** will help the dog get well.

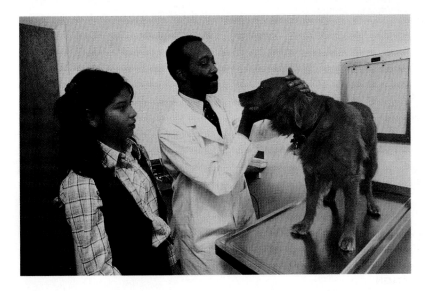

Wet

I got very **wet** in the rain.

ACKNOWLEDGMENTS

The publisher gratefully acknowledges permission to reprint the following copyrighted material:

"Cat Kisses" by Bobbi Katz. Copyright © 1974. Reprinted with permission of author, who controls all rights.

"Isn't It Strange?" by Leroy F. Jackson from POEMS TO SHARE. Copyright © 1990, 1937 Checkerboard Press. Reprinted by permission of Checkerboard Press.

Illustration
Annie Lunsford, 6–7; Katie O'Leary, 8–9; Frank Asch, 10–32; Daniel Del Valle, 33tr, 62br, 63t, 63cr, 92br, 120br, 121tr; Rita Lascaro, 34, 94, 122; Eldon Doty, 35, 123; Jason Wolff, 36–37; Bernard Adnet, 38–61, 62tl, 62cr, 95; Doug Roy, 64; Ken Bowser, 65, 137; Loretta Krupinski, 66–67; Ken Spengler, 68–91, 93tr; Kim Fernandez, 96–97; Pat Cummings, 98–119; Esther Szedegy, 124–125; Nancy Tobin, 136; Richard Hull, 138–139; Felipe Galindo, 145, 151; Holly Jones, 144, 147; John Carozza, 148, 150.

Photography
10: t. Jan Asch. 33: b.l. PhotoDisc. 38: b. Courtesy of Bernard Adnet. t. courtesy of Kirchoff/Wohlberg , Incl; 68: t.r. Photo by Kent Lacin. 68: t.l. Courtesy of the author. 93: b.c. Richard Hamilton Smith/Corbis. 93: b.r. Richard Hamilton Smith/Corbis-Bettman. 98: t. Photo by Percidia. 99: r. Nuridsany et Perennou/Photo Researchers. 99: l. L. West/Photo Researchers. 99: m. Stephen Dalton/Photo Researchers. 99: t.r. Corbis-Bettman. 99: t.l. PhotoDisc. 101: L. West/Photo Researchers. 105: Nuridsany et Perennou/Photo Researchers. 109: b.r. Corbis-Bettman. 113: b.r. PhotoDisc. 117: b.r. Stephen Dalton/Photo Researchers. 121: b.r. PhotoDisc. 135: b.r. Ken Cavanagh. 143: Pete Turner/Image Bank. 144: b. Karl Weatherly/Corbis. 145: Pete Turner/Image Bank. 146: Francis Westfield. 146: b. Steve Grubman/The Image Works. 147: Berenholtz/The Stock Market. 148: b. Jaime Villaseca/Image Bank. 149: t. Renee Lynn/Tony Stone. 150: b. Stock Market. Spengler Creations/Kent Lacin. 151: Mike Malyszko/PNI/Stock Boston.

READING FOR INFORMATION
All photographs are by Macmillan/McGraw-Hill (MMH); and Ken Cavanagh for MMH except as noted below.
Photography
140: Ariel Skelley/The Stock Market.